Around the World

Homes

Margaret Hall

Heinemann
LIBRARY

www.heinemann/library.co.uk
Visit our website to find out more information about Heinemann Library books.

To order:

 Phone 44 (0) 1865 888066

 Send a fax to 44 (0) 1865 314091

 Visit the Heinemann Library Bookshop at www.heinemann/library.co.uk to browse our catalogue and order online.

First published in Great Britain by Heinemann Library, Halley Court, Jordan Hill, Oxford OX2 8EJ, a division of Reed Educational and Professional Publishing Ltd. Heinemann is a registered trademark of Reed Educational and Professional Publishing Ltd.

OXFORD MELBOURNE AUCKLAND JOHANNESBURG BLANTYRE
GABORONE IBADAN PORTSMOUTH (NH) USA CHICAGO

Designed by Lisa Buckley
Originated by Dot Gradations
Printed in Hong Kong/China

ISBN 0 431 15122 9 (hardback)   ISBN 0 431 15127 X (paperback)
06 05 04 03 02   07 06 05 04 03 02
10 9 8 7 6 5 4 3 2   10 9 8 7 6 5 4 3 2 1

British Library Cataloguing in Publication Data
  Hall, Margaret
    Homes - (Around the world)
    1.Dwellings - Juvenile literature 2.Architecture, Domestic
    I.Title
    728

Acknowledgements
The publishers would like to thank the following for permission to reproduce photographs: Demetrio Carrasco/Tony Stone, pp. 1, 10; Wolfgang Kaehler, pp. 4a, 5, 21, 26; Keren Su/Tony Stone, p. 4b; Sharon Smith/Bruce Coleman, Inc., p. 4c; David Young-Wolff/Tony Stone, p. 6; Wendell Metzen/Bruce Coleman, Inc., p. 7; David Hiser/Tony Stone, p. 8; Jean Dragen/Tony Stone, p. 9; Ric Ergenbright, p. 11; Horst Baender/Tony Stone, p. 12; Lescourret/Explorer/Photo Researchers, p. 13; Jame Nelson/Tony Stone, p. 14; Bill Bachmann/Photo Edit, p. 15; John Beatly/Tony Stone, p. 16; Patrick Rouillard/The Stock Market, p. 17; John Warden/Tony Stone, p. 18; Jason Laure, p. 19; Kenneth Fink/Bruce Coleman, Inc., p. 20; Paul Chesley/Tony Stone, p. 22; Vince Streano/Corbis, p. 23; Sue Cunningham/Tony Stone, p. 24; Adrian Murrell/Tony Stone, p. 25; Tony Stone, p. 27; Martha Cooper/Peter Arnold, p. 28; Nigel Hillier/Tony Stone, p. 29.

Cover photograph reproduced with permission of David Hiser/Tony Stone.

Every effort has been made to contact copyright holders of any material reproduced in this book. Any omissions will be rectified in subsequent printings if notice is given to the publishers.

Any words appearing in the text in bold, **like this**, are explained in the glossary.

Contents

People have needs

People everywhere have the same **needs**.
They need food, clothing and water.
They need to be able to get from place to
place. All around the world, people also
need somewhere to live.

4

Where people live makes a difference to what they eat and wear and how they travel. It also makes a difference to their homes.

Why people need homes

People need homes as **shelter** from the sun, wind, snow and rain. Homes keep people warm in cold weather and cool in hot weather.

Homes give people a place to store their belongings. They are places where people can safely eat, sleep and be together.

Homes around the world

Homes are built in many sizes and shapes. They can be made from wood, bricks, **concrete** or stone. They can even be made from mud, grass or old tyres.

People build homes to suit the **climate** in their part of the world. They use **materials** that grow or can be found where they live.

Homes for cold places

Some places get very cold in the winter. People who live in those places need homes that **protect** them from the snow and wind.

People who live in cold places need to keep warm. Their homes usually have fireplaces or heating. They may have thick walls and special roofs and windows to hold the heat in.

Building cold-weather homes

Thick forests grow in many cold **climates**. Wood from these forests is often used to build warm homes. People also use stone, brick and **concrete** as building **materials**.

In cold climates, there can be lots of snow. Cold-weather homes often have steep roofs that stick out. The heavy snow and ice can slide off the roof and away from the house.

Homes for hot, wet places

In **tropical climates**, people need **shelter** from the sun, heat and rain. They need houses that let air inside to keep them cool.

Some homes in hot, wet places do not have walls. Others have **shutters** that keep out sun and rain but let in cool breezes.

Building hot-weather homes

Many trees and plants grow in **tropical climates**. People often build their homes from wood. They may weave leaves or grasses together to make roofs.

Floods are common in hot, wet places.
Sometimes houses are built on **stilts** to
keep them above flood waters. Being high
off the ground keeps the houses cooler, too.

Homes for deserts

Deserts are very dry places. Days are usually hot, and nights can be cold. Desert people need homes that **protect** them from the sun, heat, wind and cold.

Thick walls help desert homes stay comfortable in hot and cold weather. Houses are often built with cool, shady **courtyards** in the middle.

Building desert homes

There is very little rain in **deserts**. Not many trees grow. Desert homes are not usually made from wood. Some are made with mud walls and straw or grass roofs.

Other desert homes are built out of **adobe** bricks. These building **materials** would fall apart in wetter places.

Homes for many people

In cities, there is not enough land to build houses for every family. Lots of people can live in large blocks of **flats**.

Sometimes people from many families decide to live in a group and share a home. Older people may live together so they can be cared for by others.

Makeshift homes

Sometimes people do not have enough money to buy building **materials**. They have to build homes from things that other people have thrown away.

People may build homes from metal, cardboard or scraps of wood. These homes do not have electricity or running water.

Homes that move

Nomads are people who move their **herds** of animals from place to place to find fresh grass. They need homes that they can take with them. They live in tents that can be folded and carried.

Other people live in houseboats, on the water. Sometimes they work in their houseboats, too. Some houseboats are like floating shops where other people buy things.

Special homes

Some people build houses that are far from cities and towns. This one is made of mud and old tyres. It is warm in winter and cool in the summer.

People make their homes in all kinds of places. Some people live in caves. No matter what they look like, homes are **shelter** for the people who live inside them.

Photo list

Glossary

adobe mixture of earth, straw and clay that is dried in the sun

climate weather in an area throughout the year

concrete man-made material that changes from a thick liquid to a rock-like solid

construction building

courtyard part of a building that is surrounded by walls but has no roof

desert dry place with very little rain

flat home in a building with a number of other homes in it

flood overflowing water

herd group of animals, such as sheep, cattle or goats

makeshift something made without much planning from whatever can be found

materials things that can be used to make something

needs things people must have in order to live

protect keep safe

shelter place to keep safe

shutter movable cover for a door or window

stilt post that supports a building above the ground or water

transport ways to move people or goods from place to place

tropical hot and rainy

More books to read

Houses by Godfrey Hall, Hodder Wayland, 1999

I Live Here by Bill Boyle, Heinemann Primary, 1991

Let's Build a House by Mick Manning and Brita Granstrom, Franklin Watts, 2000

The True Story of the Three Little Pigs by John Scieszka, Puffin, 1991

This is Our House by Michael Rosen, Walker, 1998

Index

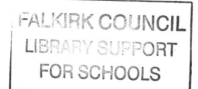

Titles in the *Around the World* series include:

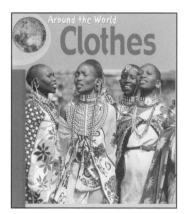

Hardback   0 431 15120 2

Hardback   0 431 15130 X

Hardback   0 431 15121 0

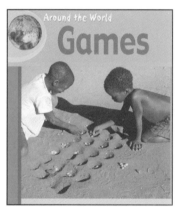

Hardback   0 431 15131 8

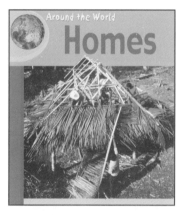

Hardback   0 431 15122 9

Hardback   0 431 15132 6

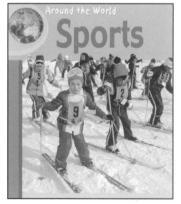

Hardback   0 431 15133 4

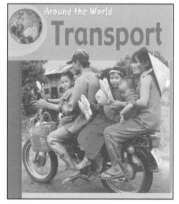

Hardback   0 431 15123 7

Find out about the other titles in this series on our website www.heinemann.co.uk/library